AFRICAN ELEPHANTS

SUNBIRD
PUBLISHING

First published 2000
2 4 6 8 10 9 7 5 3 1
Sunbird Publishing (Pty) Ltd
34 Sunset Avenue, Llandudno, Cape Town, South Africa
Registration number: 4850177827

Publisher Dick Wilkins
Editor Brenda Brickman
Designer Mandy McKay
Production Manager Andrew de Kock

Reproduction by Unifoto (Pty) Ltd, Cape Town
Printed and bound by Tien Wah Press (Pte) Ltd, Singapore

ISBN 0 62403 845 9

TITLE PAGE *The African elephant can only survive in areas where the habitat is
still intact to cater for its demanding needs. Water plays an integral part in the
elephant's life, and they not only drink copious amounts of it, but derive a great
deal of enjoyment from splashing about, and even swimming in it.*
LEFT *A family of elephants quench their thirst at a water hole.*
OPPOSITE *Two bulls. The elephant on the right is testing the wind for signs of
the presence of man or possibly a large carnivore.*

Introducing African elephants

'The long-term survival of elephant in many, if not most, countries in Africa will ultimately depend upon the cooperation and goodwill of the people who live alongside them. Without their support and their realisation of any long-term benefits from wildlife, the battle will be lost. We live in a world where man has stretched out his hand to touch the stars, where he has left his mark upon the dark, dim world of the ocean floors and where the most inhospitable parts of the earth hold no fears for him. Our responsibility is to prove that man does still care about wild creatures and wild places. That we are not limited by large or small commercial considerations but that we have the vision to pass this world and its creatures to the care of our children in a better condition than we found it.'

BELOW *Elephants are dependent on water and will drink regularly, consuming as much as 100 litres at a time.*

Wise words, indeed, and from a man who has spent many years in pursuit of the conservation of Africa's elephants. Author and scientist, Anthony Hall-Martin has dedicated much of his life to the study of elephants: their characteristics, behaviour and breeding patterns, and much of what is today common knowledge stems from his seemingly tireless efforts to discover and record every facet of elephant life.

Elephants are essentially gregarious creatures by nature and may be found in groups of anything between 10 and 20 or up to 50 or more, and, in rare cases, in excess of 100. However, elephant behaviour varies from area to area, although their highly developed social structure remains consistent throughout their distribution. Family units are led by a cow elephant, or matriarch, and a typical family herd consists of cow elephants of varying ages: the leader, – usually the oldest cow – and her sisters, their daughters and offspring. Whether members are related or not, the herd functions as a close-knit unit. When a bull reaches puberty, his time within the herd comes to an end, although he may return or join other herds for short periods. As an adult, he will not remain with any family herd permanently.

Experts differ in their estimates of the amount of food consumed by the average bull elephant, but all agree that it is well over 100 kilograms a day, and the search for sufficient grazing and browsing may take an elephant over several kilometres at a time. Areas through which a feeding herd has passed can be clearly picked out, even by the inexperienced eye: trees stand stripped of bark and leaves, branches are snapped or torn off and whole trees are often pushed over in an attempt to reach tender foliage on the upper branches.

ABOVE *Constant touching and reassuring of one another is common in elephant relationships.*

Elephants prefer to stay close to water and it is usually the vegetation that is within close proximation of water holes and pans that suffers most damage, especially in dry periods when elephants congregate at water points in large numbers. Fortunately, after the rains when water becomes more plentiful all around, the elephants disperse, giving plant life a chance to recover.

The trunk, which is a highly sensitive organ, is the elephant's lifeline, and is used for smelling, food gathering, drinking, and as a weapon. Water is drawn up through the trunk and as much as 100 litres may be consumed at a time. Elephants are dependent on water although they can go for a number of days without it. They drink regularly, when they can, and will go to great lengths to dig for fresh sources. It goes without saying that they are extremely fond of bathing and wallowing in mud and water.

Some people assume that the larger an elephant's tusks, the older the animal. This is not always the case. Tusks are nothing but a set of overgrown incisor teeth; the first set appears when a calf is about two years old and, like a human child's milk teeth, these soon drop out to be replaced by permanent teeth. From then on the tusks continue to grow until death, but in some individuals the growth is rapid, in others slow. Aside from these incisors, elephants have six sets of molars that come into use one after the other. Naturally, the daily consumption of masses of plant material takes its toll on these broad, flat, grinding back teeth. Once a set of molars becomes worn, it drops out and a new set moves forward to take its place. Research indicates that the first set drops out and is replaced by the second when the elephant is about a year old, and the sixth and last set moves into position around the forty-fifth year. Once the final set becomes worn, the elephant's days are numbered: feeding becomes increasingly difficult and the animal's condition deteriorates until, eventually, it dies.

Below The enjoyment experienced by this family group of elephants at a water hole is evident.

It is a common misconception too that only bull elephants carry tusks. In fact, cows also carry tusks, although they are perhaps smaller and less impressive than their male counterpart's incisors.

Even regular game park visitors find it difficult to tell male and female elephants apart by outward physical attributes only, except, of course, when the bull's penis is erect. However, there are specific characteristics that divide the two sexes. For one, the elephant cow's head is angular in shape – clearly discernable in profile – while the bull's is far more rounded, probably resulting from having to carry heavier ivory. I have seen tourists, once they have become aware of this difference, able to distinguish quite easily between a bull and a cow standing near each other and both offering a side view, but at a loss to determine the sex of a solitary elephant, which does not offer the comparison.

By the time a bull elephant is 30 years old, he will usually have developed certain unique physical characteristics that make him easily identifiable. Often the shape and condition of his ears will be a dead give-away. Whether tattered ears are the result of numerous fights or simply injuries sustained over the course of years in the wilds, no two elephants damage their ears in exactly the same way. Similarly, no two elephants carry identical tusks. Scars on the body offer yet another method of positive identification. Some elephants, too, adopt unique habits and can often be told apart simply on this basis.

Elephants have a long gestation period: 22 months. The newborn calf, weighing some120 kilograms, is small enough to fit comfortably under its mother's ample belly and for a few months it will spend much of its time in this safe spot. Even when the herd is moving – which it does at the pace of its slowest member – the little one will be safe, running along between its mother's legs at first and, when it is older, beside or right behind her. The cow's mammary glands are situated well forward between her front legs because the calf suckles

Above Elephants spend between 16 and 18 hours a day eating, and consume well over 100 kilograms of both grass and browse.

with its mouth. Initially it has to make quite an effort, stretching with all its might to reach them. At this stage the calf has no idea of the usefulness of its trunk and, until it begins to discover its manoeuverability and functions, this clumsy appendage tends to get in the way at times. The efforts of a very young calf trying to keep its trunk from interfering with its suckling can be very amusing, especially when the calf gives vent to its annoyance with shrill squealing. The same happens when at first a calf attempts to drink water. Until it masters the skill, its attempts are accompanied by indignant squealing and foot stomping – for all the world like a petulant human toddler.

Because a calf is totally dependent on its mother until it is about two years old, there is a gestation interval of at least three years. Cows usually guard over their first-born closely, but calf-rearing is a fulltime task, and by the time the mother bears her second or third calf, she seems to have no qualms about temporarily delivering her offspring into the capable care of another cow. Such a 'nanny' is often one of the younger cows that has not yet given birth herself, and tending to another's youngster will stand her in good stead in a few years time when she has one of her own. Frequently a calf will have a favourite cow to which it turns for attention, much like the indulgent aunt in a human family! Like our own children, elephant calves progress through various distinct stages of development as they get older, all with the function of preparing them for the roles they will perform as adults. Cow calves are less adventurous and, it would seem, less mischievous than their boisterous young 'brothers'. When elephants descend on a pan or water hole, they do so not only to drink but to swim and, joy of joys, to wallow. While older elephants tend to go

BELOW Elephants drink daily and will go to great lengths to dig for water using both their tusks and feet.

about their routine somewhat more sedately, the calves rush right in to roll and wriggle gleefully in the thick mud. This is their playtime and while very young calves continue to keep close to their mothers, the older, more confident ones get up to all sorts of mischief, delighting in teasing one another as well as any other creatures in the vicinity.

On many occasions I have been entertained by the comical sight of a stroppy calf, imitating the actions of an irate adult, charging a warthog or an antelope. At the slightest suspicion of danger, however, it will dash right back to the safety of the herd – to be enticed, before long, by the sight of yet another 'innocent victim'.

After the first year the varying character traits of bulls and cows become more apparent. Young bulls acquire an awareness of the importance of their position among peers and begin tentatively to test themselves against one another, engaging in games of mock fighting and mock charging. As their confidence increases, their behaviour towards one another becomes more openly challenging. Mock charges are performed with a flourish and, as happens with human children at play, at times matters threaten to get out of hand. At this point, an adult will usually intervene, placing a restraining trunk between the two rivals as if to say 'enough is enough'. And, surprisingly, the calves cease their scuffling.

Just before bull calves reach puberty, their rivalry becomes intense and often they pair off, practicing their fighting skills. By their fourteenth or fifteenth year young bulls leave the herd, but may remain together for a while still. I have seen such groups, just recently part of a family herd, on the grassy plains near Savuti marsh in northern Botswana, and by then their play fighting had taken on a sharper edge. Previously it had been simply a game, a necessary progression within the confines of the herd; now it had to do with establishing a ranking among them. Soon they would begin to drift apart, separating to go their own way. Sometimes a young bachelor may join an older bull

ABOVE A pair of desert-dwelling elephants of the Kaokoveld, now a part of Namibia's Kunene Province, cross a riverbed.

but, even with the old gentleman not averse to a bit of company, they will not remain together for long.

Cow elephants breed throughout the year and if a lone bull should come across a group of cows, he will certainly ascertain whether they are in oestrus. If not, he may chose to remain with the herd for a while anyway, to socialise.

Unlike males of many other species, bull elephants are quite tolerant of one another. Should two bulls meet at the same water hole, the tension is usually relieved by one acknowledging his subservience. This is achieved by placing the tip of the trunk in the mouth of the dominant bull; almost immediately the tension seems to dissipate and they will drink and wallow side by side in peace. I have, on occasion, seen two physically well-matched bulls simultaneously place their trunks into each other's mouths; I do not know whether this meant that they regarded themselves as equals. Perhaps they knew each other very well and the mutual gesture served simply as a greeting, but I liked the idea that two such enormously powerful animals would prefer to conduct themselves peacefully for the few hours that they shared the waters of the pan.

Of course, fighting does erupt at times, inevitably when there are cows in oestrus. Normally a few mock charges are sufficient to convince one bull of the other's dominance and only when neither is willing to relinquish dominance, or when a dominant bull takes offence at the other's proximity to, or interest in a breeding cow, will a confrontation result in fighting. Initially the bulls will engage in severe mock charges; an awesome sight, with each trying to look as imposing as possible. Raising themselves to their full height, ears flaring and cracking like a whip, the bulls kick up dust and trumpet shrilly, to electric effect. During the last moments of a mock charge, the elephants will stop short, only a few paces apart. Should neither be willing to back down, they retreat and charge again, repeating the performance a number of times before they meet each other head on. The power and vibrancy of the moment is indescribable: the sound of clashing tusks and snaking trunks leaves no doubt as to the seriousness of the fight.

BELOW In the dry season, elephants will cover great distances in their search for water.

Deep wounds are often inflicted. Bulls in musth are highly aggressive and will inflict fatal wounds on other bulls, so it is not surprising that they are given a wide berth by other elephants. Musth (or must) refers to the periodic states of frenzied sexual excitement experienced by the males of certain large mammals, especially elephants. It is associated with a discharge from the gland between the ear and the eye. Any elephant bull with a noticeable discharge from these glands should be treated with the utmost respect and caution. Most fighting, however, takes place when an elephant's survival is threatened. Elephants find themselves under great stress during times of drought or at the end of a long, dry winter. Seasonal clashes between bulls are a frequent occurrence at water holes and chips of broken tusks are a common sight. The elephants become irritable in their desire for clean water: shoving, growling and bellowing in their attempt to get at it.

I have spent more than 30 years in the pursuit of elephants; my passion for these giants knows no bounds. However, one should always recognise that they are potentially dangerous and one should always, if on foot, approach elephants with the greatest of caution.

Nonetheless, anyone who has spent time observing a herd of cow elephants with their calves will agree that it is one of the most heartwarming experiences in the wild. Apart from testy old bulls, which for the most part seem to prefer a solitary existence, elephants are social animals. There is sufficient evidence too to prove beyond doubt that they are highly intelligent and highly sensitive. Physical contact as well as communication is important. Elephants seem constantly to be touching and 'talking' to one another, using a wide variety of sounds and movements. Squealing, grunting, sighing, even the flick of an ear seems to communicate a message of some sort. Certainly the trunk is used to convey affection, subservience, and even irritability; to subdue an overexcited calf, or soothe a frightened one.

ABOVE A matriarch leads her family in single file across calcrete-dotted ground to a water hole at the edge of Etosha Pan.

When working in the Tuli Block in the 1960s, I was intrigued when observing a large group of elephants within the thick riverine vegetation alongside the Shashi River, to see all the elephants come to an abrupt halt, ceasing whatever activity they were at that moment involved in, regardless of whether they were pulling a branch down, had food in their mouths or were walking forward. With one accord all the elephants remained perfectly still and silent, and I pondered as to what in fact was taking place. I ventured to suggest that a telepathic system existed among elephants. After pausing for a period of time, all the elephants would, on some unheard signal, continue on their way. Years later I was to learn that the amazing work carried out by Katy Payne, an American naturalist who had specialised in music and biology at Cornell University, had been studying the vocalisation of elephants over a period of many years, when she and two colleagues discovered that elephants in fact use infrasound – a sound below the range of human hearing. An amazing revelation about an animal that has roamed planet earth for at least 45 million years!

ABOVE   A cow and her calf enjoy the lush grass on the plains beneath Mount Kilimanjaro. Note the slender tusks and pointed head of the females.

ABOVE RIGHT   A cattle egret *(Bububulcus ibis)* enjoys a ride, possibly taking the opportunity to feed on insects disturbed by the elephant's movement through the grass.

OPPOSITE   Three bull elephants on the open plains of Amboseli National Park, Kenya. The seasonally lush vegetation of this 365-square-kilometre park, backed by the magnificent snow-capped Mount Kilimanjaro, is one of the finest in all Africa, and hosts an estimated population of more than 800 elephants.

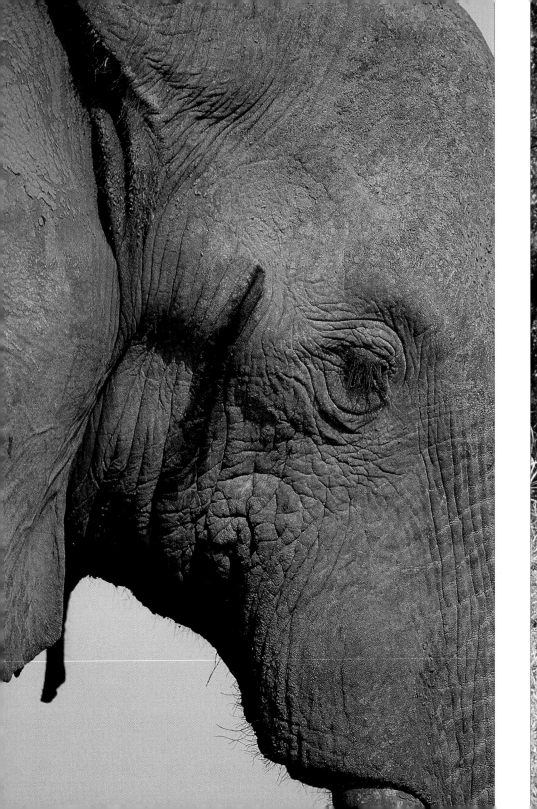

PREVIOUS PAGES A bull elephant displaying all the symptoms of musth. Apart from the visible discharge from the temporal gland, the gait of an elephant in musth is noticeably different, and there is a continuous dribbling from the penis, which can be observed running down the sides of the back legs and also from the unsheathed penis. Bull elephants in this condition are extremely aggressive towards other males.

LEFT The trunk, a highly sensitive organ, is the elephant's lifeline, and is used for smelling, food gathering, drinking and even as a weapon. This large bull elephant is endeavouring to reach the upper branches of a fever tree *(Acacia xanthophloea).* Elephants are able to rise up on their hind legs in their efforts to reach the highest of branches.

ABOVE Elephants are quite capable of modifying their environment when forced to remain in a particular area. The whole question of elephant habitat 'destruction' has arrested the attention of wildlife managers and biologists for decades. The debate falls into two areas – those who believe in the systematic removal of elephants and those who believe in a laissez-faire policy of live and let live.

OPPOSITE A solitary bull elephant makes his way across open grassland in Kenya's Amboseli National Park. Seeing an elephant such as this one out in the open is a reminder that a central element of why these animals have captured our minds is, of course, their sheer size. The elephant dwarfs us and reminds us of our own fragility.

LEFT A young elephant cow with her calf. After a 22-month-long gestation period, a single calf is born. The birth of twins, while extremely rare, has been known to occur.
OPPOSITE A family group comprising cows and calves slakes its thirst at a water hole in Hwange National Park. The trunk is used not only to draw up as much as four litres at a time, but also for spraying the body with water in order to cool the elephant down. Elephants will often take a dust bath after bathing, which may act as an abrasive in order to keep the skin healthy and prevent blood-sucking insects from bothering them.
OVERLEAF LEFT AND RIGHT A newborn calf weighs in at about 120 kilograms and is small enough to fit comfortably under its mother's belly. This calf is suckling from its mother, whose mammary glands are situated between her forelegs.

PREVIOUS PAGE LEFT An elephant exhibiting the typical motions of a mock charge: rocking with one foot swinging to and fro, and shaking the head with a loud slapping of the ears.
PREVIOUS PAGE RIGHT A family line of elephants heading across a Zambezi flood plain at Mana Pools in Zimbabwe.
RIGHT A herd of buffalo (Syncerus caffer) waits patiently in the background while an elephant herd dominates a water hole. Elephants are known to drive other animals away when they occupy a watering point, and these buffalo will invariably wait patiently until the elephants have satisfied their thirst, or fulfilled their desire to wallow and play in the mud.

OPPOSITE A group of bull elephants following the dry Rhunde riverbed that snakes its way through the Chilojo cliffs in Zimbabwe's Ghonarezhou National Park. It is not unusual to find groups of bulls in bachelor herds. Whilst they do split up, when they rejoin they quickly identify one another, generally living a life of peaceful coexistence. When musth occurs in one or another of the elephants, they quickly assume the dominant role and separate themselves from the group.

OVERLEAF LEFT AND RIGHT Elephants, especially the youngsters, are extremely fond of bathing and wallowing in mud and water and take great delight in shoving one another around and climbing onto each other's backs. Bathing is essential to an elephant's skin care, at the same time effectively cooling the body.

ABOVE Tusks are nothing more than an overgrown set of incisor teeth, and they occur in both male and female African elephants, as opposed to their Asian counterparts where only the bull elephants carry ivory. Tusks are used in sparring, for gouging bark and digging up roots, and represent a formidable weapon when an animal defends itself or attacks another animal apart from its own kind.

RIGHT Although elephants are essentially grass eaters – grass comprises up to 80 per cent of their daily diet – they also consume a wide variety of other vegetation, including leaves, bark, roots, wild fruits, and seed pods of various species which they swallow whole. They use both the trunk and tusks to acquire these foodstuffs.

LEFT Elephants are extremely adept at sucking up water and mud and then, with a backward swing of the trunk, are deftly able to splash the mud and water across the back of their ears and shoulders.

ABOVE Apart from using the trunk to cover their bodies with mud and water, they kick their forelegs rapidly into the mud, effectively wetting their under body parts.

OPPOSITE A young elephant is seen here splashing mud and water onto its right ear and eye area. The body temperature of an elephant is maintained by hot blood passing through large arteries and veins located on the surface of the back of the ear. The constant fanning of the ears is probably also a contributory factor in cooling the blood as it circulates through the arteries and veins before returning to the body.

OVERLEAF LEFT Two bull elephants tolerate a herd of impala *(Aepyceros melampos)* at a water hole in Botswana. Solitary bulls and bachelor groups are far more tolerant of animals than are herds of elephants, especially when young elephants – who are in the habit of teasing other species and constantly chasing them off – are present.

OVERLEAF RIGHT A giraffe *(Giraffa camelopardalis)* bears witness to two young bull elephants sizing each other up in Chobe National Park, Botswana. Bull elephants will often stand in water for long periods at a time, almost as if they are in deep meditation. Without warning, one may suddenly lurch towards the other, or fling his trunk out.

ABOVE LEFT AND RIGHT Elephants thoroughly enjoy a dust bath. The trunk is used to suck up a large amount of sand which is then forcibly expelled through the proboscis over the animal's body. They rapidly take on the colour of the earth found in their area: the elephants of Tsavo National Park in Kenya are 'red', while elephants of Etosha National Park in Namibia are very pale in colour. After the onset of the rains, or a good swim in the river, they rapidly return to their original hue of slate grey.

OPPOSITE Like a large ghostly ship sailing through fog, an elephant skirts a water hole at dusk.
OVERLEAF LEFT A herd of elephant along the Khwai River area in Moremi Game Reserve. Moremi forms part of the great Okavango Delta in northern Botswana. Next to Zimbabwe, Botswana has one of the largest concentrations of elephant in Africa.
OVERLEAF RIGHT A lone bull elephant crosses the Linyanti River, which forms part of the boundary between Botswana and the eastern section of the Caprivi Strip of Namibia.

THIS PAGE AND OPPOSITE Cow elephants and their calves in the Eastern Cape's Addo Elephant National Park, South Africa. Addo represents the last stronghold of the Cape elephant, which was all but exterminated by the turn of the century. The park, proclaimed in 1931, has in excess of 300 elephants, and plans are afoot to further expand Addo – which has increased seven-fold over the last decade – to incorporate seven major vegetation types. The park already enjoys a rich diversity of plant life, making it one of the best small elephant parks in Africa.

OVERLEAF LEFT AND RIGHT One of the finest places in Africa to view elephants is the Savute in Botswana's Chobe National Park. The Savute channel flows eastwards out of the Linyanti swamp via the Zibadianja Lagoon, finally emptying itself out into the 108-square-kilometre Savute marsh, a distance of over 100 kilometres. Here, prior to 1982 when the channel ceased to flow, water was available over an uninterrupted distance covering the full length of the channel. Concentrations of wildlife along the length of this channel were impressive, not least the vast numbers of elephants that congregated here during the dry season. Today the channel is bone-dry back to the Linyanti and it is only through the placement of artificial water holes that elephants are able to remain in this area during the dry season.

THESE PAGES AND OVERLEAF LEFT Bathing, even when there is a plentiful supply of water, is not necessarily a daily ritual. A good soak, however, is generally welcomed after a long day's foraging and there is no doubt that elephants really enjoy themselves in the water. These giant animals will often immerse themselves completely, with just the trunk protruding from the surface. Elephants will often spend a great deal of time at a muddy water hole in their efforts to get at the clean water closest to the surface, and will brush the water from side to side before drinking.

OVERLEAF RIGHT After a long drink and a mud bath, these two elephants stand placidly side by side. After drinking and bathing, elephants will often move off a short distance and then proceed to 'dust' themselves before finally moving off.

PREVIOUS PAGE LEFT Two young bull elephants approach a water hole in Etosha National Park, Namibia. Note the short or broken tusks, which are characteristic of elephants in this part of Africa. Due to the extremely dry climate, the ivory is brittle and is easily broken either when elephants go head to head or in their daily foraging where the tusk is used. Measuring some 21 346 square kilometres, a large part of which comprises the Etosha Pan, the park is regarded as one of the most spectacular in Africa. Etosha boasts a population of approximately 2 000 elephants. Fountains and boreholes on the perimeter of the pan provide the water necessary to sustain life in an area that is known for its low rainfall.

PREVIOUS PAGE RIGHT AND OPPOSITE A family group approaching a water hole in Etosha National Park, Namibia. After a long hot day, elephants will often break into a run over the last 200 to 300 metres, and the approach to a water hole by herds of elephant is sometimes heralded by trumpeting and bellowing. This particular group is very placid as it calmly approaches water, now almost line astern with the largest cow in the front, the youngsters tucked in behind the mother and aunts.

OVERLEAF LEFT AND RIGHT Two bull elephants in Etosha National Park, Namibia. Note the massive size of the elephant on the right (page 47) and the characteristic short ivory that is common in elephants from this area. Elephant bulls, when habituated to the presence of motor vehicles, are relatively easily approached, enabling one to obtain good photographs of these magnificent creatures. Apart from Etosha, elephants are to be found in Namibia's Caprivi and the Kunene Province, which includes both Damaraland and Kaokoland, home to the famed desert elephants. In historical times, elephants occurred from south of the Sahara all the way to the Cape. The last century has seen a catastrophic decline from an estimated population of 1.2 million in 1977 to around about 600 000 African elephants today. Although good ivory is generally absent from elephants from this part of Africa, it is their ivory that has been the principal cause of their decline. With the advent of the arrival of sophisticated automatic weapons onto the African continent in the early 1970s and 1980s, the fate of the African elephant was all but sealed until 1990 when an international ban on the trade of ivory was enforced, thus providing a vitally needed pause in order to let populations recover in many of their former ranges.

PREVIOUS PAGE LEFT This young elephant is throwing dust up onto its back, using sideways motion as opposed to the other method of flinging the trunk back over the head and then expelling the dust onto the shoulders, neck and flanks.

PREVIOUS PAGE RIGHT It is not uncommon to see a young elephant placing browse on its head. They have an amazing sense of humour and appear to enjoy amusing themselves.

ABOVE AND RIGHT A group of bull elephants at a water hole at Savute, Chobe National Park, Botswana, with a number of skittish impala (Aepyceros melampus) and female kudu (Tragelaphus strepsiceros) present. Apart from the presence of predatory lions (Panthera leo), and possibly the black rhinoceros (Dicornis bicornis), bull elephants are generally very tolerant of other wildlife at a drinking hole. They can, of course, be extremely aggressive towards each other, which is possibly the reason for the nervousness on the part of the impala.

OPPOSITE A large bull elephant, ears erect, slakes his thirst at a water hole in Etosha National Park, Namibia, while a group of gemsbok (Oryx gazella), zebra (Equus burchellii) and a lone giraffe (Giraffa camelopardalis) wait patiently in the heat of day to move in after the bull has departed.

OVERLEAF LEFT A black rhinoceros (*Diceros bicornis bicornis*) eyes an approaching elephant at a water hole in Etosha National Park, Namibia. This subspecies of the black rhinoceros is found within the Etosha National Park, as well as in the Kunene Province's Damaraland and Kaokoland. It formerly occurred in the northern parts of the Cape Province and in southern Angola, but during the 1970s and early 1980s, numbers were reduced to a pitiful few. Successful translocations of the species from Damaraland in the 1970s enabled the authorities to re-establish this species in Etosha National Park, where they have adapted extremely well. Elephants will endeavour to intimidate rhinos, which give way with a lot of huffing and puffing, at a water hole.

OVERLEAF RIGHT After a long hot day feeding out in the blazing sun, and at the prospect of a long, cool drink, elephants cannot resist running the last few hundred metres to a water hole. When water is readily available, elephants will drink daily and may consume as much as 220 litres at a time.

ABOVE AND RIGHT Cow elephants are extremely protective of their offspring, and the bond between a mother and daughter will endure for her entire life. With the popularity of wilderness trails in many parts of southern Africa, contact with breeding herds of elephants is inevitable and one has to exercise the greatest caution when in close proximity to these animals. A matriarch or a member of her clan will not hesitate to attack any intruder they believe may threaten the family group, and this can result in dire consequences for the intruder.

OPPOSITE An adult cow elephant with her latest calf, flanked by a second calf, which in all probability is also hers. Note the very pronounced mammary glands between the adult cow's forelegs.

LEFT AND ABOVE Even though these two elephants are of comparable size, the elephant above has virtually no tusks, while this Kruger National Park bull is a magnificent tusker. Bulls carrying good ivory are usually to be found in areas affording them excellent protection. However, in the case of the Etosha's elephants, where they also enjoy good protection, it is more a question of the brittleness of the ivory in relation to the climate and possibly the quality of the water they are forced to drink. By contrast, bulls in the Kunene Province to the west are known to carry better ivory, but then again they live in a colder, less dry climate.

OPPOSITE A magnificent lone bull elephant in the grasslands of Tanzania's Ngorongoro Crater. Large ivory-bearing elephants were prime targets for ruthless poachers who decimated Africa's elephant populations in the 1970s, 1980s and early 1990s. The recent upsurge in the poaching of African elephants is cause for some concern.

OVERLEAF LEFT Drinking is a social event among elephants and they will often be found packed shoulder to shoulder. When they have satisfied their thirst, a herd will move away together. This family group it at a water hole in Etosha National Park, Namibia.

OVERLEAF RIGHT Elephants will go to great lengths to drink the cleanest water they can find. However, in times of drought and when large numbers of animals congregate at water holes, they don't always have a choice. They will often stand for long periods at a time, gently moving the water from side to side with a stroking motion of the trunk and then sucking up the clear water on the surface.

OPPOSITE This lone bull elephant plods gently down the dry Hoanib riverbed alongside the towering rocky buttresses that are a characteristic of this river, flanking it on both sides. Evidence from rock engravings and written records indicate that there have been elephant in this desert region of the Kaokoveld since time immemorial – an indication that they were not driven into the desert by human disturbance or pressure. These desert-dwelling elephant have developed their own gene pool characteristics, including their uncanny ability to precisely locate a fountain of water out in the middle of nowhere, as well as the physical attributes such as the sharply up-curved tusks found in the bulls.

THIS PAGE The desert-dwelling elephants of the Kaokoveld – now known as the Kunene Province, Namibia – along with the black rhinoceros, are the jewels in that arid world's crown. They are a dimension of added grandeur and excitement found nowhere else in Africa. During the 1970s their numbers declined dramatically and at one point they were in danger of extinction through indiscriminate poaching. Through the timeous intervention on the part of leading non-governmental organisations and the official conservation agency of what was then known as South West Africa, poaching was halted and the species has, during the past two decades, made good progress in its recovery. The Kaokoveld was divided into two regions, Damaraland in the south and Kaokoland in the north. The Hoanib Valley, where these elephants were photographed, is the dividing line between these two zones. These elephants are well adapted to living under the particular ecological conditions of this desert. They routinely move great distances – up to 70 kilometres – between feeding grounds and the scattered water holes where they drink during the dry season.

LEFT FROM TOP TO BOTTOM Bulls feeding on the dominant ana tree *(Faidherbia albida),* found on the Hoanib Valley floor.

ABOVE The mountains of the Kaokoveld are characterised by deep gorges, extremely narrow, razor-sharp slopes, rugged ridges and dry riverbeds. Elephants here are heavily dependent on the vegetation of these riverbeds for food.

OPPOSITE Travelling upwards of four days at a time between water holes, these elephants are able to eat plants that are totally unpalatable to other animals. Because food sources are widely scattered, the elephants venture out into these trackless wastelands from one riverbed to the next, and built into their incredible memory bank is the precise location of a fountain or a pool containing water.

OVERLEAF LEFT Elephants follow well-worn paths established over decades leading from one river to the next. When disturbed or frightened, they have an amazing ability to move quickly over these rock-strewn landscapes.

OVERLEAF RIGHT A herd moves in single file across the Hoarusib Valley. The Hoarusib River rises in the Ovahimba Highlands to the northeast of Kaokoland. The major rivers of the Kaokoveld all flow from east to west – from areas of higher rainfall through areas of decreasing rainfall – until they end in the desert dunes of the Namib. From time to time, the Hoarusib River reaches the sea, thus carrying water into the desert in surface flow or under the sand, which in turn enables a chain of vegetation typical of the high-rainfall areas to reach further into the inner Namib and as far as the coastal desert itself.

LEFT AND BELOW An elephant's trunk hardly ever remains still, other than when the animal might be dozing in the heat of day. Apart from its principal function of enabling the animal to feed and to drink, this amazing appendage is not only a useful tool with which to cover the body with mud (which not only cools the body but discourages irritating flies), but acts as a marvellous snorkel when the animal is submerged in a river, and is a wonderful instrument for scratching, for balancing when resting on one tusk, and for greeting other elephants. It is also very effectively used as a devastating weapon, and the sideways blow from an elephant's trunk is not something from which one is likely to recover. The combination of trunk, tusk and foot activity is nothing short of astonishing, and I have seen large slabs of concrete lifted off French drains in an elephant's efforts to get at water.

OPPOSITE This elephant, swimming in a river in the Kruger National Park, holds the trunk aloft – possibly it has detected a strange scent and is inquisitively trying to ascertain what or who it might be. Elephants are incredible swimmers, employing a dog-like paddle while holding the trunk aloft, and have been known to cross great distances even in deep water where they are unable to stand.

PREVIOUS PAGE LEFT A solitary bull elephant etched against the rugged escarpment of the Hoanib Valley. Note the characteristic upward curve of the tusks. The shrub layer in the background forms part of the riverine vegetation, comprising locally dense thickets, in this case of the *Salvadora persica,* or mustard tree.

PREVIOUS PAGE RIGHT Sharing this ancient landscape with the elephants are the Himba people, whose deserted village lies beyond the passage of this family group of elephants. The remains of Stone Age cultures are widely scattered throughout the Kaokoveld. In historical times, the dominant people of Kaokoland have been the Herero-speaking Bantu ethnic groups. It is in their language that the name of the land and its greatest river have their origins. It is said that when the Herero moved southwards into the Kaokoveld from their ancestral homelands in Angola, in about 1550, the Kunene River was on their right, or to the northwest, so they called the river Okunene, meaning the right arm. The land to their left they called Okaoko, from which Kaokoland takes its name.

PREVIOUS PAGE LEFT Two mature bull elephants size each other up while standing knee deep in water. The elephants are evenly matched, although the one on the left is slightly disadvantaged because of its broken tusk.

PREVIOUS PAGE RIGHT Other than when an elephant is in musth, sparring and fighting among bull elephants is not usually a serious affair. These elephants are 'trunk wrestling', with a great deal of pushing and shoving.

LEFT A family group of elephants displays aggression and excitement at the presence of wild dogs at a kill, and is clearly intent on chasing the predator off.

BELOW LEFT AND RIGHT Elephants are highly intelligent animals and the presence of a dead kudu in all probability has been heightened by the awareness and scent of the nearby lions, which have either skulked away or have been driven off. Elephants show a particular interest in the dead of their own kind, and will walk up to an elephant carcass and run their trunk over the body in the most gentle and touching manner or, in the case of a skeleton, have been known to pick up bones and tusks and carry them off for some distance.

OPPOSITE A bull elephant in a mud hole in Savute, Chobe National Park, confronts a pack of wild dogs by flinging his trunk out and holding his ears erect, at the same time standing tall. Large carnivores invariably elicit some form of aggression or threat from elephants.

PREVIOUS PAGE LEFT Holding its trunk aloft, this young elephant is endeavouring to locate the source of its interest. Elephants' sense of smell is acute and they have good hearing. However, their eyesight is poor, and providing one stays perfectly still and the wind is in your favour, you will remain undetected. They have, however, the added advantage of being able to communicate through infrasound and, in all probability, have alerted the others within the herd to the possibility of imminent danger.

PREVIOUS PAGE RIGHT Sociable behavior within elephant society is extremely important, especially when two elephants approach one another, in this case in a greeting ceremony. While it can often take the form of trunk entwining, these two have gone trunk to trunk, with tusks are interlocked. In lower-ranking animals, the tip of the trunk is inserted into the mouth of the oncoming dominant bull.

LEFT An elephant in the Kruger National Park endeavouring to reach the browse of a marula tree *(Sclerocarya birrea)*. Using its trunk, an elephant can reach heights of up to six metres. For an animal that requires anything between 150 and 200 kilograms of food a day, it is not surprising that it employs its trunk, tusks and feet in an effort to satisfy this hunger.

OPPOSITE The elephant is the world's largest land mammal, and in the case of a large bull, weighs in at anything between 5 000 and 6 000 kilograms, standing at a height of between three and 3.4 metres. At this size, it is understandable that, when feeding, these huge animals will invariably push over and break down trees. When elephants are confined to relatively small areas this can lead to the destruction of the habitat. Elephants will utilise as much as 90 per cent of the local plants, and their diet ranges from bulbs, tubers, aquatic plants, sedges, grasses and fruits, to roots, flowers, bark, seeds and even whole branches of trees.

THIS PAGE AND OPPOSITE Elephants have a simple digestive system and do not chew their food finely, passing as it often does, through their system little changed.

OVERLEAF LEFT The tusks of an elephant are no more than enlarged upper incisors. The elephant throughout its lifetime has six sets of cheek teeth, two in the lower jaw and two in the upper jaw. As the animal grows older, these increase in size and move into place as each successive set wears out. Ultimately the elephant, once it has used up all six sets, will die of starvation.

OVERLEAF RIGHT The mopani tree *(Colophospermum mopane)* is one species of which elephant are particularly fond and the leaves are rich in protein and phosphorus. This elephant, with its head enmeshed in a shower of leaves, is endeavouring to dislodge its next mouthful by means of the end of its trunk. If undisturbed, or not on the move, elephants will often remain for a lengthy period of time at one particular shrub or tree until they are satisfied and will then move on to the next plant. This elephant has a fine pair of tusks, of which at least a third penetrate up into the jaw below the eyes. Each tusk has a long fish-shaped nerve extending down the tusk. Should the elephant break its tusk off at the lip and expose the nerve, this can cause immense discomfort.

OVERLEAF LEFT When elephants put on a threat display they advance with ears held out like large sails, and the head held slightly back. Thereafter they invariably turn aside with back arched and tail held high. Bull elephants when threatened, hurt or angry, are capable of charging up to speeds of 40 kilometres an hour, but in most cases it is shear bluff in order to scare one off.

OVERLEAF RIGHT Young males practising their fighting skills while at the same time establishing their position within the hierarchy of bull society.

ABOVE This young tuskless elephant is caught in the act of browsing and looks somewhat curious as to the intrusion. The ears held erect, with one foot raised, indicates an alert posture.

RIGHT Covered in mud, this young elephant has chosen a convenient termite mound to give itself a well-deserved belly rub. Termite mounds, rocks, tree trunks and embankments are all utilised by elephants as scratching posts.

OPPOSITE Young elephants spend a great deal of their daily activity at play, shoving, pushing and sliding, especially in mud holes and river sand. If the situation gets out of hand, they may be reprimanded by either their mother or an aunt.

ABOVE Elephants are known to ignore standing water and will go to great lengths to dig alongside it in order to obtain clean water.

ABOVE RIGHT This elephant is shaking the trunk of a real fan palm *(Hyphaene benguellensis)* in the Okavango Delta, Botswana, in order to dislodge its fruit. Elephants are extremely fond of the fully ripened, dark, glossy brown fruit.

OPPOSITE An excavated hole in a dry riverbed in the Kruger National Park during the drought provides relief to these elephants, one of which bears a remarkable set of tusks.

OVERLEAF LEFT Two young elephants quench their thirst in the Kruger National Park.

OVERLEAF RIGFT The trunk is used to suck up water, and is then lifted, the tip inserted into the mouth, and the water released to sate the elephant's thirst.

PREVIOUS PAGE LEFT A breeding herd, having slaked its thirst, returns to the scrubland that is its home. The habitat of the Addo Elephant National Park is unlike any other in Africa, dominated largely by succulent green plants that provide a rich food source.

PREVIOUS PAGE RIGHT Having first quenched her thirst, this elephant is now indulging in a free-for-all kicking and trunk-slapping match, clearly delighting in what has now become a game.

LEFT TOP TO BOTTOM The antics of young elephants are heart warming. These two young elephants are engrossed in covering themselves in soft mud. They seem capable of amusing themselves for hours on end, and are quick to rush into play with a sibling or cousin.

ABOVE AND OPPOSITE Trunks entwined, two young elephants of roughly the same age indulge in a bout of play fighting. The tear in the right ear of the elephant on the left may have been caused by the nip of a sharp tusk or branch. This behaviour is part of the growing-up process. For males, pushing, shoving and head butting are a necessary part of their development, and will ultimately prepare them for their eventual position in the hierarchy structure of bulls. When they reach the age of between 12 and 14 years, they become sexually mature and will move away from the herd, having by now become thoroughly disagreeable as far as the adult females in the herd are concerned.

LEFT When very young, the ears of an African elephant appear to be out of proportion when compared with the size of its body, and at this age, when the ears have not yet turned over, they look for all the world like two large sails. This young elephant – in all likelihood still suckling from his mother – is busily engaged in picking up a branch and play eating.

ABOVE Two young elephants hungrily browsing on a thorny bush. Thorns present no problem to either elephants or rhinos, and they will readily demolish them, thorns and all.

OPPOSITE A tightly packed group of tuskless elephants from Addo Elephant National Park with their attendant offspring. The youngest elephant in the centre is, in all probability, only a few months old, and will stay very close to its mother. At birth, calves stand at about 85 centimetres tall at the shoulder, and are covered in a dense coat of black hair that disappears with time.

THIS PAGE Elephants are excellent swimmers, and from a very early age, have no hesitation in entering water. This elephant (top left) is sliding down into the water, with its back legs splayed out behind it. Even adult elephants will adopt this posture when they are not altogether certain of their footing and have been known to slide down the dunes in Namibia's Skeleton Coast Park in similar fashion. Water holes such as that illustrated here can present a serious problem to very young elephants, who can get mired down in the mud, requiring the efforts of the mother and attendant aunts to pull the animal free. These older elephants are clearly not concerned for their own safety in any way and are entirely consumed by the absolute joy of playing in water.

OPPOSITE A good swim presents these two young elephants with an excellent opportunity of testing their strength in shoving and pushing each other around, while at the same time developing bonds that will last throughout their lifetime. If their play becomes too boisterous, they are soon sorted out by the adult females. Elephants are highly intelligent animals, and much of their long lifespan – up to 60 years – is, not unlike a human's, spent in learning.

LEFT This photograph clearly illustrates the close bond that exists between cow and calf, and indeed within all elephant society – the close proximity of the mother and the baby, and the trunk of another elephant placed gently across the youngster's head.

ABOVE Protectively flanked by its mother and an aunt, the extent to which elephants will go to protect their young is clear, especially at times when they are out in the open near water, and the presence of lions might present a threat.

OPPOSITE The Addo Elephant National Park was proclaimed in 1931, following a conflict with agriculturalists that resulted in the shooting of some 120 Cape elephants, and in an effort to preserve what was left of this decimated elephant population. The solution, provided in 1954 by Graham Armstrong, was the erection of an elephant-proof fence, comprising railway lines and cable that surrounded the original 2 200-hectare reserve. Today some 330 of these animals roam freely in a park that is continually increasing in size.

The love and care a mother elephant bestows on her calf is no more or less than that offered by females of the human species. Mother elephants will protect their young ferociously, and will go to extreme lengths to ensure their offspring's well-being. Calves will suckle from their mother for many years, even though they will generally be independent of their mother's milk after some two years.

ABOVE AND RIGHT Elephants are extremely agile and are equally at home in a variety of habitats – from the African savanna to the slopes of mountains and the dunes of deserts. Here they stand placidly at a water hole, negotiating a mud wallow. They are also extraordinarily mobile for animals of such huge proportion. In June 1218 BC Hannibal left Cartagena (Spain) to attack Rome from the north. The purpose of his expedition was to relieve the endangered city of Carthage. In November of the same year he arrived at the Alps with 38 000 footmen and more than 8 000 horsemen. Departing from the Rohn River, he arrived on the plains of the River Poe 15 days later, with only 14 000 soldiers and 6 000 horsemen. At the outset of this journey, this formidable force was accompanied by 37 elephants; at the journey's end, these same 37 elephants were all present and accounted for.

LEFT AND ABOVE Tusks occur in both male and female elephants. However, in the case of females, the tusk tends to be more slender and to weigh less than that carried by males. It is not uncommon to come across tuskless females, an occurence that is extremely rare in the case of bulls. Apart from their use as an effective weapon, they assist greatly in feeding. While of obvious use to the elephant, ivory has almost led to the creature's demise. Man's preoccupation and passion for ivory goes back thousands of years, although it is only in the last 150 years that we have seen the impact on Africa's elephant populations, reaching its zenith in the early 1990s. In 1989 the species was listed as 'endangered', which has greatly assisted in halting the downward spiral of their numbers throughout Africa.

OPPOSITE Making their way slowly through the low scrub vegetation of Addo Elephant National Park, a herd of tuskless females leads the family to water. A bull elephant brings up the rear. As elephant numbers rebound, they present new challenges for park managers as elephants are quite capable of modifying their environments – to the detriment of not only themselves, but to the biodiversity of the parks within which they roam. South Africa is unique in Africa in that all of its elephants are to be found in fenced areas (a fact that encourages environment devastation by the elephants). Possible solutions to controlling elephant populations are many, but controversial. Increasing habitat areas can become a very costly business, and the capture and removal of family groups is difficult, especially in the case of eco-specific elephants such as those at Addo, and even the effectiveness of culling is vehemently disputed.

THIS PAGE For visitors to Africa, elephants are at the top of their game-viewing lists, and scenes such as these are indelibly etched into the mind.

OPPOSITE Elephants may sleep for anything from four to five hours in a 24-hour period, and adults generally sleep or doze while standing. Young elephants happily flop onto the ground, often at their mother's feet, lying with their own feet stretched out before them, contentedly snoring. I have witnessed adult elephants, during the heat of the day, stretched out flat on the ground taking advantage of the dense, cool vegetation. On occasions such as this, one is able to approach the sleeping elephant at close range without being detected.

OPPOSITE Two bull elephants engaged in a test of strength. These bouts are important in determining the position of an individual in bull hierarchy. Heads held aloft, trunks entwined, these bouts generally do not lead to serious injury. However, when a female is in oestrus, one or the other may suffer injury when the animals are aroused.

ABOVE AND RIGHT These young bull elephants are more likely engaged in play fighting than in the act of greeting one another. The presence of water has no doubt heightened their excitement. When greeting, they will often touch the tips of each other's trunks or touch each other about the head.

ABOVE, LEFT AND RIGHT The trunk is the nose of the elephant and has two nostrils running through its centre. The tip acts as a lip, enabling the animal to gather up food, water or dust.

OPPOSITE Elephants are essentially gregarious creatures by nature and have a highly developed social structure, led by a cow elephant or matriarch.

LEFT The water holes made by elephants provide liquid refreshment for a variety of antelope, carnivores, warthog, baboons, birds and invertebrates.

TOP The typical gait of an elephant is one of a rocking motion, with the trunk swinging from left to right.

ABOVE A young elephant trying to make up his mind whether or not he should chase off this fully grown male ostrich *(Struthio camelus).* Young elephants delight in chasing other, generally smaller, species of game.

OPPOSITE Two young elephants greet each other at a water hole by placing the tips of their respective trunks into each other's mouths.

LEFT Two subadult bulls engaged in a free-for-all, with the one elephant attempting to drive the other away from the mud bath. Elephants of this age will unite in fighting in their effort to achieve dominance. To counter persistent aggression, the victim will often turn his back to the aggressor.

BELOW A young bull attempts to force his attention on a young female, who is clearly disinterested in his advances.

OPPOSITE Two young bull elephants in a show of greeting. When they reach puberty their boisterous behaviour, in many instances, causes the older cows to drive them out. Bull elephants are known to form bonds that last well into their adult lives.

OVERLEAF Flanked by its mother and an older sibling, this young elephant is secure in its world of close family ties.

PREVIOUS PAGE LEFT A juvenile covered in mud chases a calf, equally mud-splattered, at a water hole in Addo Elephant National Park. Young elephants can become very boisterous during play and are capable of hurting one another. In this case, the older elephant is a female, and is most likely chasing the younger one away.

PREVIOUS PAGE RIGHT A bull elephant enjoys a good soaking in a water hole, eyed by an Egyptian goose *(Alopochen aegyptiacus)*. These birds regularly frequent pans that are used by elephants, bravely expressing their displeasure at this intrusion.